ORPHANED WISDOM

Meditations for Lent

✳   ✳   ✳

Michael E. Moynahan, S.J.

PAULIST PRESS
New York/Mahwah

Scripture references are from the New American Bible.

Library of Congress Cataloging-in-Publication Data

Moynahan, Michael E.
    Orphaned wisdom: meditations for Lent/Michael E. Moynahan.
      p. cm.
    Includes bibliographical references.
    ISBN 0-8091-3198-6
    1. Lent—Meditations. 2. Catholic Church—Prayer-books and
devotions—English. I. Title.
BX2170.L4M69   1990
242'.34—dc20
                                            90-41131
                                            CIP

Published by Paulist Press
997 Macarthur Boulevard
Mahwah, New Jersey 07430

Printed and bound in the
United States of America

Contents

*This book is dedicated
to Tom and Mary Mellon,
John and Linda Tidgewell,
Marie Leonardini and
Paul Belcher, S.J.
who have accompanied me
for twelve years on this
faith journey.*

This collection of contemporary poetic meditations captures the small child in all of us. Divided into the six weeks of Lent, it provides daily "food for thought" with poetic meditations on the spirit of conversion and welcomes us into the spirit of the church on retreat and the spirit of Lent as an invitation for renewal.

Introduction

Change is an essential ingredient to life. We are surrounded by reminders that people and things in life change. The seasons of the year remind us of change as we move through the mood and thermostatic shifts of winter, spring, summer and fall. Familial relationships remind us of change as we move from being children ourselves to gradually assuming the successive roles of parent, grandparent and great-grandparent. Our bodies remind us of change as our hair thins, our waistline expands, and our pace of life, however reluctantly, slows down.

We change in many ways: physically, emotionally, sexually, psychologically, and spiritually. As inevitable and important as change is, most of us are reluctant to view it positively, cooperate with it and view it as a potential friend.

Orphaned Wisdom is a book about spirituality and change. It is a book that believes we are all called by God to change and grow in our relationship with God. Change and growth for the person in relationship with God takes the shape of ongoing conversion. Anthony de Mello spoke of this in one of his earlier books. "Spirituality is that which succeeds in bringing one to inner transformation."[1]

The psalmist and the prophet, while they may never have used the word "spirituality," knew the truth that de Mello's definition captured. The psalmist puts it as a prayerful plea.

> To you, Yahweh, I lift up my soul,
> O my God. . . .
> Yahweh, make your ways known to me,
> teach me your paths.

Set me in the way of your truth, and teach me,
for you are the God who saves me.[2]

The person who is in relationship with God is first and foremost
a disciple. *Discipulus* literally means "learner." As people in
relationship with God, we are constantly learning that God's
ways are not our ways. Because we are people with short attention spans and even shorter memories, we constantly need to be
reminded. God is willing to call us over and over again to this
needed change through the prophetic voices God sends to us
throughout history. For there is one thing greater than our for-
getfulness, and that is God's memory. Isaiah's is one of those
many prophetic voices through which God calls us to "change
and be saved."

Turn to me and be saved,
all the ends of the earth,
for I am God unrivaled.[3]

The change we are speaking about, in spiritual or religious
terms, is called conversion. Basically, it means to turn back to
God's ways of thinking and God's ways of acting. Conversion is
not a product. It is a process. Conversion is not a once-and-for-
all-time event or a momentary experience. Conversion is the
daily process of every Christian's spiritual life. It is an ongoing
process. Through it we allow God to change us.

The church in its wisdom saw the necessity of such ongoing
reformation of one's life and built it into the liturgical season we
call Lent. Through Lent we once again prepare ourselves to celebrate the central events and mystery of our Christian faith: the
suffering, dying and rising of Jesus Christ.

Lent is an invitation to every Christian. It is an invitation to
conversion. For those involved in the Rite of Christian Initiation
of Adults, it is a time to come and commit ourselves to the life
and values of Jesus Christ. For those of us already baptized, it is
an opportunity for us to renew and deepen this commitment.

Lent is a time to ask some basic questions: What aspects of

our lives are in need of conversion? What values are important to us? For what are we willing to take a risk? Who or what is God in our life? Where do we find God in life?

Lent is a time to take stock. It is a time to examine our goals, our means to attain those goals, and our motives. Are they the gospel goals, means and motives of our teacher Jesus Christ? Lent is the chance to change those areas of our life in need of conversion. It is a time to reorient the direction of our life.

Traditionally, Christians prepare themselves during Lent through the three practices mentioned in the gospel reading for Ash Wednesday.[4] These three practices are prayer, fasting and almsgiving.

Orphaned Wisdom is a collection of contemporary poetic meditations that invite you into the spirit of the church on retreat, into the spirit of Lent, into the spirit of conversion. They are divided into the six weeks of Lent. Each weekday has a poetic meditation, a suggestion of a form of conversion we are being called to, and a piece of scripture that can offer you further food for thought on this form of conversion.

On the Sundays of Lent you will find Contemporary Annotations for those engaged in the spiritual life. Four friends have joined me in this part of *Orphaned Wisdom*. These Contemporary Annotations are reflections on different aspects of our relationship with God.

My hope is that these poetic meditations and contemporary annotations will assist you to change those areas of your life that God is calling you to change. They have done and continue to do that for me. As we accept another generous invitation of our God to enter into Lent and embark upon this journey called conversion, let us remember and draw hope from the words of St. Paul to the community at Corinth:

> As your fellow workers we beg you not to receive the grace of God in vain. For God says, "In an acceptable time I have heard you; on the day of salvation I have helped you." Now is the acceptable time! Now is the day of salvation![5]

NOTES

1. Anthony de Mello, *The Song of the Bird* (Garden City, New York: Image Books, 1984) p. 11.
2. Psalm 25:1, 2, 4-5.
3. Isaiah 45:22.
4. Matthew 6:1-6, 16-18.
5. 2 Corinthians 6:1-3.

Contemporary Annotations

by Sonny Manuel, S.J.

1. Remember everyone
   who has ever loved you.
   Remember everyone
   you love.

2. Gradually
   confront
   all
   that
   you
   fear.

3. Don't rush anything.

4. Regress again
   and again
   to wherever
   you feel solace.

5. Ask yourself:
   "What's important?"
   "What's urgent?"
   And wonder why.

6. Put words
   to your loneliness,
   your sadness
   and your anger.

7. Do whatever you want.

8. Do nothing.

Orphaned Wisdom

Common sense:
easy to say,
hard to do.

A thousand thoughts
bombard this battered heart.
Bloated by countless things
that promised satisfaction
and left me empty.
Where do I look for you now?
How will I know you?
When will you come?
How will you come?

Re-learn those lessons
all too quickly forgotten—
substance only slightly tasted.

Orphaned wisdom,
too long lost,
buried under tons
of less important things.
When you are hungry:
eat.
When you are thirsty:
drink.
When you are tired:
rest.
When you are lonely:
meet.
When you are angry:
talk.

When you are happy:
talk.
When you are sad:
talk.
When you are frightened
or confused:
talk.
When you are grieving
or disbelieving:
tell the story.
Listen to the story.
Listen to your story.
Listen and live.
Let the thought,
the feeling,
the sensation
find expression
the way you allow
such experiences
to become flesh and blood
of human communication.

Remember this:
more is less.
Remember this:
less is more.

Dry dusty roots,
gnarled arthritic veins,
no longer able to unwind,
to stretch out finger tips for
cleansing,
refreshing,
renewing
moisture.

Paralyzed
by self-inflicted
deserts,
you,

dew,
drop in.
You gently,
imperceptibly,
make your way
into hardened
sponges.

*　　　*　　　*

Conversion: To common sense.

Scripture: "Why spend money on what is not bread,
your wages on what fails to satisfy?
Listen, listen to me,
and you will have good things to eat . . .
listen, and your soul will live." [Isaiah 55:2–3]

A Spirit of Adventure

Get in the boat.
Don't take out the oars.
In fact,
throw them overboard.
Let the water carry you
where it will.
Be surprised.
Getting tense?
Does the suspense
kill you?
Relax.
The current knows
where it is going.

Let the child within
out.
Let that parched
and starving urchin
inhale a spirit
of adventure.
You're off!
You're out
of your cotton-picking
mind!
Give that humor-less,
over-protective parent
a sedative.
Resist the temptation
to direct,
to steer clear of
mystery.

And if you get
the urge
to jump in
and test the waters,
don't resist.
Surrender.
Remember:
the water is
as buoyant in seventy feet
as it is in seven.

To appreciate
the voyage from shore
to our first "resting point"
you'll need
an understanding heart.
Wait a minute!
Heads understand.
Hearts feel.
This just doesn't
make much sense.
It requires more than
linear thinking.
A friend of gentle wit
once quipped:
"If you want logic,
worship a computer."
Bon voyage!

❋　　　❋　　　❋

Conversion: To leave what is known and journey into mystery.

Scripture: "God said to Abram, 'Leave your family and your father's house, for the land I will show you.'"
[Genesis 12:1]

Count On It

Boastful God,
you deliver
as much and more
than you promise.
Would you be considered
cost effective?
In the shadow
of a fluctuating
Dow Jones average,
can we describe you
as a good risk?

Magnanimous God,
you want us
to have it all
but not
all at once.
You patiently wait
until we are ready
for each of your
endless gifts.

God of knowing gaze
and wisened smile,
you watch us spend
some forty odd years
wandering in the desert.
How can you smother
laughter as you watch us
struggle unsuccessfully
to have what we want?

Gently teach us
now
to want
what we have.

＊　　　＊　　　＊

Conversion: To trust in a God who cares what happens to us.

Scripture: "Do not be afraid, for I am with you." [Isaiah 43:5]

New Life

The promise
of new life:
new blood flows
in tired veins.
Twelve months
seems small change
to pay
for what
I'm given
in return.

What do you want?
I want . . .
I want a healthy child.
No matter
whether male
or female.

And what would you
name this child?
God is faithful
to his promises?
God is with us
still?

The name of this child?
Here and now.
Bit by bit.
One step at a time.
Do the next thing
you have to do.

The name of this child?
Whole-hearted.
Engager.
Jumper-into-life.
No matter how large,
no matter how small,
no matter how brief,
no matter how long,
no matter how important,
no matter how insignificant,
do it
with your
whole heart.

The name of this child?
Enjoy-able.
As simple as
one, two . . .
(what comes after two?)
Able to enjoy.
Eating, drinking,
sleeping, waking,
in sickness or health,
in plenty or poverty,
in sorrow or joy,
in the desert
or on the mountain top,
living or dying,
able to delight
in the moment
you're given.
It's the only one you have.

The past a phantom
wisp of smoke
that no longer exists.
The future a dim
distant shadow.
Where you are,
what you have

is
here
and now.
Bingo!
A light goes on.
Bells ring.
It's jackpot time
in Tahoe.

Jump in.
Enjoy.
This moment
is brought to you
by someone
who cares.

✳   ✳   ✳

Conversion: Openness to new life.

Scripture: "Know this too: your kinswoman Elizabeth has, in her old age, herself conceived a son, and she whom people called barren is now in her sixth month, for nothing is impossible to God." [Luke 1:36–37]

What Is It Time For?

A parable
for pilgrims
featuring a monk,
a monastery,
a reporter,
a tolling bell
and haunting question.

Reporter.
"In this day and age,
why do you live
so removed
from the world?"

Monk.
"There's a story
buried deep
beneath
each action,
each question,
each thought,
each feeling,
each experience had,
every person met."

Monastery.
"The only place
to find
the one you seek
is here and now,

wherever you are,
whatever you're doing."

Vox fabulae.
(The challenge
and the promise
of the pregnant
present moment:)
"Come to me
completely,
with your doubts
and with your clarity,
with your thoughts
and your distractions,
with your pleasing
and confusing feelings,
with your promises
made and forgotten,
with your commitments
kept and broken,
with your dreams
lost or shattered,
with your body
well worn and long past
the warranty,
with your spirit
drained and wounded,
and I will heal you,
and renew you,
and disclose myself
to you."

Stunned reader.
"Hey, wait a minute!
Where did that voice come from?"

Tolling Bell.
"Bonnnngggg! Bonnnngggg!"

Haunting question.
"What is it time for?"

✳   ✳   ✳

Conversion: To find God in the present moment.

Scripture: "Be still and know that I am God." [Psalm 46:10]

Forget-You-Not

You show-
(and tell)
stopping
oak tree
with elephantine trunk
I cannot
completely
embrace.
Summer evening's
light and I
have learned
an occasional caress
must suffice.

You hand of God,
grounded
with muscle-toned
fingers
stretching,
twisting majestically,
each in its own way
pointing out
incarnated mystery.
Together,
one mighty,
open palm of praise.

Plenty of room
to lie down
and rest in it.

✳   ✳   ✳

Conversion: To believe in the faithfulness and love of God.

Scripture: "I will never forget you. I have carved you on the palm of my hand." [Isaiah 49:15–16]

Contemporary Annotations

by Michael E. Moynahan, S.J.

1. Pay attention
   to everything.
   I said:
   Pay
   Attention
   To
   EVERYTHING.

2. Hindsight is worth having.
   Don't forget to turn around
   and look at what's been happening
   from time to time.

3. Deserts are filled
   with quiet life.
   So,
   Shut up!
   Look!
   Listen!
   And enjoy.

4. We ask for a product
   and are given a process.
   The constant response
   to all our questions
   and objections?
   "Come and See."

Fearfully Wonderfully Made

Adversarial thinking:
Is it this
or is it that?
Yes!
Boyle's First Law.

You give me
a good eye
to see humor
in the big
and little
paradoxes
of life.

You give me
gentle wit
and laughter
that help me
weather storms,
certain balm
for self-inflicted
wounds.

You give me
imagination,
that aikido way of
looking,
seeing,
thinking,
being.
(Don't resist,
deflect.

Reflect.
Honor the energy
and direction
of others.
Let them lead you
to uncovered possibilities,
constantly present but
unlooked for things.)

You give me
creativity:
writing,
playing,
clowning,
cooking.
Remember:
The watched pot
never . . .
Boyle's Second Law.

You teach me
how to shake-
and-bake stories:
Weaving words
into a web of
hospitality,
forcing people
willingly
to come close
around the fire,
warming hands
and hearts.
Flinching.
Inching
our
independent
ways
cautiously
closer
into

community.
Tales told
that mesmerize us
and in this
spell-bound state
force us to let
that captive child within
out.
Ring
around the
dragnet.

You give me
your eyes.
You share
the secret
of looking for
and finding
buried beneath
layers of debris
your tell-tale
signature:
mudcaked goodness.

You give me
your heart
so I can
gently hold
the incarnated mystery
of your little ones.
Beware of gifts
bearing peeks.
Boyle's Third Law.

✳   ✳   ✳

Conversion: To embrace the humor in life.

Scripture: "There is a season for everything, a time for every occupation under heaven . . . a time for tears and a time for laughter . . ." [Ecclesiastes 3:1,4]

Aerial Mentor

As the last, bland
grains of sand
slip out of my
hour of power
prayer-glass,
an aerial intruder
arrives.

Only a pane
of clear glass
separates us.
Is it a window
looking out or in?

Eyeball to eyeball.
Beak to beak.
A spunky little
humming bird's
body language
boldly declaring:
"Now,
have I got
your attention?
Watch this and
remember it good,
Bozo!"

Hovering there
I wonder:
Do you ever go hungry?
Dinner time now.
Feasting on what those

red and pink and
peach and purple
flowers hold.
(No squeezing blood
from turnips here!)
Tasting
what is there
to eat and drink
and moving on
to the next moment,
the next meal,
the next flower
somewhere
further up
the road.

*　　　*　　　*

Conversion: To listen and learn from nature and the animal world.

Scripture: "Look at the birds in the sky. They do not sow or reap or gather into barns; yet your heavenly Father feeds them. Are you not worth much more than they are?" [Matthew 6:26]

Broken Record

In the matter of our
teatime infidelities,
you're no apparent parent.
You refuse to treat
them with that ultimate
seriousness
that is its own
reward.

We cart around
our peccadillos,
little "i" dolls
for show-and-tell.
Each of us a
Robert DeNiro
(in The Mission)
carrying all that baggage
around our necks
like cabbages
weighing us down.
It makes
the monumental task
of mounting cliffs
sheer madness.

So,
what's in
the bag?
Let it out.
Failures?
Unfulfilled promises?

Unrealized potential?
Faith broken?
Friendship betrayed?
Chances never taken?
What do we really fear?
We fear success.
For then we'd have
to hold a garage sale
and part with all those
musty images of self
that have gathered dust
since childhood.

What's your response
to our bragging contests
and comparison of scars?
("You think that's bad, eh?
Well just take a look
at this one.")
Forgiveness.
(Water on a westward witch.)
Forgiveness
yesterday,
today,
and wonder of wonders,
(thank you, Annie)
tomorrow.

Grandparenting God,
you see our sin as
symptomatic stutter,
self-effacing struggle
to ignore
the confounding reality
of your willful
vulnerability:
"I love you
because I can't do
anything else.
I made you,

every last part of you:
all that's hidden
and all that's revealed,
all that's muddled
and even all that's clear.
You are,
at the risk
of repeating myself,
dear to me.
You are precious
in my eyes
because . . .
just because
you are mine.
That's enough for me.
And it will have to do
for you.
Wrestle with it
until you get tired
and then relax
and give in.
Take a deep breath
and enjoy.''

✳   ✳   ✳

Conversion: Belief in the forgiving love of God.

Scripture: "All day long I hope in you
because of your goodness, God.
Remember your kindness, God,
your love that you showed long ago.
Do not remember the sins of my youth;
but rather, with your love remember me."
[Psalm 25:6–7]

Redemption Center

A model home:
a place for everything
and everything in its place.
No creased couch cushions,
no crystal chipped,
no newly tarnished silver,
no faucets leaking,
no unsightly bathtub rings,
no closet mothball fragrance,
no sagging beds,
no pillows minus
feather luster,
no weather worn windows
or swollen doors.
Everything is perfect.
Only one slight
problem:
no sign of being
lived-in.

My home:
plaster peeling,
furniture whose
springs are sprung
and stuffing spent,
walls that sport
unsightly shiners
and toothless smiles.
If only nicks
could chat.
You have to have

the knack
of reading between
the scratches.

O God,
our frequent bed
and breakfast guest,
why is it that
the well worn shoe,
the wrinkled shirt,
the rickety house,
and flawed coin
are always worth more
to your educated eye?

＊　　　＊　　　＊

Conversion: To joyfully embrace the human condition.

Scripture: "We are only earthenware jars that hold this treasure, to make it clear that such an overwhelming power comes from God and not from us." [2 Corinthians 4:7]

The Price Is Right

"Win over,"
not bludgeon, beat,
berate, bombard or bully.
Why is it you catch more flies
with honey than with vinegar?

"Conquer,"
that triple crown winner:
directionless, deceptive, dark.

"The Way,"
your guide and
invitation to safari.
Now that can be confusing
when the path we want
(that predictable straight line,
the shortest distance
from "A" to "B")
is not an offering
on your travel menu.

"Truth,"
the host
you won't find working
on a used car lot.
What you see is
what you get.
Now that's the problem.
The more you see,
the more you get.
And there's always more
to see.
Get it?

"Light,"
your traveling companion,
in whom there is
no darkness.

"Suffering,"
that unrelenting toothache:
relinquishing control
and doing it
your way.

"Glory,"
that thrice confounding
mystery:
companion,
helper,
and ultimate
destination.

Those fateful words,
"Come on down,"
have brought you to
this time,
this place.
Decision time now.
What are you
going to bid
on this showcase?

✳   ✳   ✳

Conversion: To look for that spark of divinity that dwells in humanity.

Scripture: "The Word was made flesh,
he lived among us,
and we saw his glory,
the glory that is his
as the only Son of the Father,
full of grace and truth." [John 1:14]

Incarnation

We tried in so many ways
to communicate our love.
If communication is not
what you say but
what people hear,
then what we said
was warped and wrenched
into distancing prescriptions
that had no heart.

You asked for food.
We sent manna.
You asked for drink.
Water flowed from the rock.
You asked for directions.
Moses brought the law.
And on and on.
Still you grew
more distant,
more deaf,
more blind.
Memories dulled.
Speech slurred.
Dreams dissolved
into wander dust.

And so we did
what families do
when confronted
with calamity.
We drew straws.

Shorty lost.
He came to share
your plight,
your fight,
your fright,
your night,
and point you
toward tomorrow.

＊   ＊   ＊

Conversion: To look at life through the mind and heart of God.

Scripture: "In your minds you must be the same as Christ
Jesus.
His state was divine,
yet he did not cling
to his equality with God
but emptied himself
to assume the condition of a slave,
and became as men are . . ." [Philippians 2:5–7]

Contemporary Annotations

by Leo Rock, S.J.

1. *Killing Time*

How do I kill time?
Let me count the ways.

By worrying about things
over which I have no control.
Like the past.
Like the future.

By harboring resentment
and anger
over hurts
real or imagined.

By disdaining the ordinary
or, rather, what I
so mindlessly
call ordinary.

By concern over
what's in it for me,
rather than what's in me
for it.

By failing to appreciate what is
because of might-have-beens,
should-have-beens,
could-have-beens.

These are some of the ways
I kill time.

Jesus didn't kill time.
He gave life to it.
His own.

2. *Nothing Is Happening*

"How is it going?"
"Okay, I guess.
But nothing is
happening."

If that seed,
fallen into the ground,
could speak,
I can hear it say:
"Nothing is happening."

The mountains,
in their majesty:
"Nothing is happening."

The sea
becalmed:
"Nothing is happening."

Like me,
in the still quiet
of myself:
"Nothing is happening."

Check Out Time

So wise
for one
so young.
Your badly barren cousin
carries new life
within her,
or so the angel claims,
as she heads toward those
twilight years.
Sounds like Rod Serling
scripted this scenario.
The signpost up ahead
reads: Barren Beth's
Amazing Abode.

How do you substantiate
a rumor of angels?
So nothing's impossible?
Maybe yes.
Maybe no
one in their right mind
would fall for that line.

You're blest because
(as preposterous as it sounds)
it happened.
And if it can happen to her
(over the hill),
it can happen to you.
You're blest because
you've got common sense.

You know what confirmation is
and how to get it.
Since that character
was speaking truth,
a trusted friend
can use some help.

A trip in time saves
peace of mind.
A pilgrim approach
to "check it out":
the proof is
in the plodding.

＊   ＊   ＊

Conversion: To understanding God's ways.

Scripture: "Glory be to God whose power, working in us can
do infinitely more than we can ask or imagine."
[Ephesians 3:20]

In the Out House

It's been a long,
dusty ride.
A steep and winding road
weaves serpentine
up the side of mountains.
They race the sun
with prospects of a new head to tax,
albeit a small one,
an impending certainty.
Sky and mother
are visual proof.

They reach the city
exhausted
but full of hope.
The husband,
mistaken on occasion
for her father,
fails to act his age
and dashes toward
a door about to close.

"Excuse me.
Could you give us
a room for the night?
Some place to lay our heads?"

"Can't you read, buster?
We're all filled up."

"I understand.
It's my wife.

She's about to have
her first child."

"That's not my problem."

"He's not a problem.
He's a fact
of life."

"Open your ears, buddy,
because I'm only
gonna say this once.
We ain't got no room.
So scram!"

"I understand"
is drowned
by the sound of a
slammed door.

Three times he will try
to find them lodging.
And with each failure
feel less capable
of caring for his wife
and that life within her
wanting out.

"It doesn't look good.
All their rooms are taken."

"Don't worry.
God will provide."

And all the time thinking:
"That's what I'm afraid of.
They're sorry
but they're full.
It's looking bleak."

"God will give us
what we need."

He shakes his head.
She believes this
and it comforts him little.

The third stop
looking like a
distant bleak relation
of the previous two.
Until the owner's wife
spies the young girl wince
from movement she understands
all too well.

"You can have
the place out back.
It isn't much,
but it will be a roof
over your heads.
There's fresh hay thrown.
The animals won't bother you
and the child will be warm.
I'll get some rags and water.
Go on now,
the mother
and baby
are waiting."

Silently
the young girl's face
proclaims:
"Magnificent!"

＊　　　＊　　　＊

Conversion: To believe in the providence of God.

Scripture: "God, forever faithful,
gives justice to those denied it,

gives food to the hungry,
gives liberty to prisoners.

God restores sight to the blind,
God straightens the bent,
God protects the stranger,
God keeps the orphan and widow."
    [Psalm 146:6–9]

Interlude

The pattern of life
is Jacob-like
in form,
if not
in content:
twenty years,
more or less,
between blessings.

Lots to show for it.
Wives married,
children reared,
flocks gotten
the old-fashioned way
(we stole them),
possessions amassed,
kingdoms built,
all water
under the bridge.

And if that first
blessing belonged
to someone else,
perhaps the doubt and pain,
that dark underbelly
of stolen beatitude,
by rights,
was theirs
as well.

An all night wrestlemania
with that stranger

(What was his name?)
leaves you
with a bruised hip
and changed name.
No longer the confusion
of question or declaration
("Who is like God")
but the haunting challenge
of a new relationship:
"Amicus meus."

God, you come uninvited,
the unexpected guest
whose intrusive gift is
"Texas-style"
hospitality.
"Y'all come back
again.
Y'hear?"

*　　　*　　　*

Conversion: To the unexpected ways God can break into our life.

Scripture: "Continue to love each other like brothers and sisters, and remember always to welcome strangers, for by doing this, some people have entertained angels without knowing it." [Hebrews 13:1–2]

In Manner Ordinary

Ever emerging God,
you are part and parcel
of that unpretentious
paschal process
as we inch our way
in caterpillic crawl
toward your glory:
becoming fully human.
What went on
those thirty
(almost unrecorded)
years between Christ's
birth and baptism?

What did he learn
from Mary?

Listen to every creature,
great or small,
for each is a story
of God.
Each has something
to speak
to welcoming ears
and open hearts.

He gleaned his first
healthy images of God
hanging around his mother:
nurturer, healer,
gentle, playful,
tender playmate,

appreciative audience,
affirmer of goodness,
forgiver of imperfections
only the strange eye
could see.

He gathered symbols
thrown around the house:
yeast, salt, light,
misplaced coins,
the hundred things
spring cleaning
annually reveals.
All carefully stored
within imagination's cupboard.

What did he learn
from Joseph?

Trust your dreams,
your intuitions,
your images,
even when calmer,
cooler minds contend
it doesn't make
much sense.
Things that confound
the head
often speak to
the heart.

When judging character
know how to ask
the right questions.
How do you pick good wood?
What will you be asking
it to do?
Which kind can give
itself uniquely
to all you ask of it?
Different woods for

different tasks.
Don't build on sand
unless you're at the beach.
A general contracting rule:
"build on solid ground"
and your creation
will stand the tests
of weather, seasons and time.

What did he learn
from his life in Nazareth?

Meals and stories
are life's staples.
Discover the rhythm
of each day,
the orchestration
of changing seasons,
the way a person's life unfolds.
Let your lively mind record
the magic of creation:
lilies of the field,
birds of the air.
Not knowing where
the next meal or drink
will come from,
oblivious to danger
lurking around the corner,
unconscious of those
disappointments
just beyond the horizon,
these unthinking creatures
somehow escape
acid indigestion.

Taste your people's poverty,
their mourning and rejoicing,
their laughter and their tears,
their dreams and disappointments,
their hope in God.

Trust the images that come from
God only knows where.
Share the stories
of childhood:
release them
so they can grow
in people's minds and hearts
igniting imagination
and new hope.

Growing up is
like a visit
to a zen garden.
Pay attention
to seemingly insignificant
depositories
of human wisdom.
Listen constantly
to your heart,
that vast uncharted area
where God hides
a pirate's plunder:
happiness.
Wondering
if and when
anyone
will look.

✳   ✳   ✳

Conversion: To find the extraordinary buried deep within the
ordinary.

Scripture: "He then went down with them and came to Nazareth and lived under their authority. . . . And Jesus
increased in wisdom, and age and grace with God
and people." [Luke 2:51–52]

Behold the Clown of God

How do you follow
in the footsteps
of a classic clown?
How does a lumberjack
stumble awkwardly after
the unselfconscious moves
of a ballroom dancer?

How does one follow grace?
Preferably with a meal.
And as they broke bread
one thought haunted them:
who is this guy?
Where does this stranger's
knowledge come from?
We just now met
yet he reads us
like a favorite book
with certain pages
yellowed from
frequent visits.

What do we want?
No one's ever asked us
that one before.

What do we want?
Have you got a few years
or is this one of those
trick questions?
Say,

wait a minute.
Are we on candid camera?

His stories
ignite imagination,
rekindle fire
where only
lifeless ashes lay.
Those vacuum cleaner eyes
take everything in
gently
penetrating
even kryptonite.
That reassuring smile
releases songs
long locked
inside our hearts.
To his trained ear
it matters not
the limit of our range
is one small note.

He speaks
with hands and heart
and touches ours.
His warm and
welcoming face say,
in ways that words
would never capture,
"Make yourselves at home."
Although we've
only known
each other for
two,
few,
brief hours,
he's earned
our windworn
wayfarers' trust.
He hypnotizes,

loosens untrained tongues
and lifts
simple fisherfolk
to the heights
of poetry.

Good God,
who is this clown?

＊   ＊   ＊

Conversion: To come and see the dwelling places of God.

Scripture: "Hearing this, the two disciples followed Jesus. Jesus turned round, saw them following and said, 'What do you want?' They answered, 'Rabbi,'— which means Teacher—'where do you live?' 'Come and see,' he replied; so they went and saw where he lived, and stayed with him the rest of that day." [John 1:37–39]

Each a Different Story

Matthew's call:
a bit more educated
than the rest.
A man of the world,
a tax collector,
he knew:
how to survive,
how to get along,
how to pick and choose
his battles.
The others resented
his selection
and his presence.

Later that evening
at his house,
on his turf,
Jesus celebrated
with Matthew and company.
Quite a rogues' gallery.
(A collection
of flawed stamps
and damaged coins.)
Matthew's associates,
like himself,
ostracized
from kosher society.
He did not pick them.
He was thrown out
like garbage

upon this heap
of humanity.
(Amazing what
an artist makes from
other people's trash.)
He went reluctantly.
Contaminated companions
were better than
solitary confinement.

And then
a miracle occurred.
What started only
as idle chatter,
passing the time of day,
was suddenly transformed
into narrative trances
around this village fire.

Each one had a story.
Each one was a story.
And if he was still,
and if he listened
with ears and heart,
and if he looked beyond
the dirt and stink and
desperation carved
deeply on their faces,
each one told him
where each had been
and where each
longed to go.

❋   ❋   ❋

Conversion: To discover that every creature is a story of God.

Scripture: "Take yourselves for instance, brothers, at the time
when you were called . . . it was to shame the wise

that God chose what is foolish by human reckoning, and to shame what is strong that God chose what is weak by human reckoning; those whom the world thinks common and contemptible are ones that God has chosen—those who are nothing at all to show up those who are everything." [1 Corinthians 1:26–28]

Contemporary Annotations

by Curtis Bryant, S.J.

With the Gift of Desolation . . .

1. I understand a way
   to overcome
   reward
   as a motive.

   Desolation is a way
   to overcome
   addictions,
   compulsions,
   attempts at control,
   idols, isaacs, etc.

2. I begin to appreciate
   the difference between
   "absence" which enables me
   to stand on my own two feet,
   and "abandonment"
   which tempts me into believing
   that I must be
   self-sufficient.

3. Life presents us
   with nothing
   which may not be viewed
   as a fresh start.

4. I begin to see
   that God loves life

in its failure
as much as in its
fruitfulness.

With the Gift of Consolation . . .

1. I cry in wholehearted wonder
that God's ways are not ours.
Enchantment and surrender
are not accidents.
One is born out of
and takes nourishment
from the other.

2. In order to be enchanted,
we must be,
above all,
capable of seeing
another person.
Mere eye-opening
will not do.
Curiosity
predisposes the eye,
but the vision
must be discerning:
deep-rooted,
integral,
and clear.

3. In order to surrender
we must be,
above all,
willing to pay
the cost
to release
an untiring instinct
for migration:
a wild urge
to depart from oneself
to another.

4. Love affairs
   reveal to us
   the carefully
   concealed
   secret
   of being.

The Mother of Learning

"What do you want?"

"Actually, lots,
but for starters,
'Where do you live?' "

"Come and see."

This was not to be
the first or last time
we fell for that one.

"Come and see."

The perfect bait
for catching curiosity
and leading
salty fisherfolk
into the depths
of mystery.

"Come and see."

"But what will we do?"

"Come and see."

"But how will we live?
What will we eat and drink?"

"Come and see."

"But all we know is fishing.
How will that help us
in following you?"

"Come and see."

And on and on
through the countless faces
of wounding and healing,
betrayal and forgiveness:
feeding the hungry,
giving drink to the thirsty,
releasing captives,
preaching good news
to those who could
least afford it,
and announcing
a year of favor
from the Lord.

We slowly tiptoed
deeper into
life and death.
His constant response
to our timidity
that tantalizing challenge:
"Come and see."

And we went.
And we saw
more than we
could ever
have imagined.

＊   ＊   ＊

Conversion: **Finding God in the needs of those around us.**

Scripture: "Then the virtuous will say to him in reply, 'Lord, when did we see you hungry and feed you; or thirsty and give you drink? When did we see you a stranger and make you welcome; naked and clothe you; sick or in prison and go to see you?' And the King will answer, 'I tell you solemnly, in so far as you did this to one of the least of these brothers or sisters of mine, you did it to me.' " [Matthew 25:37–40]

Three-Wheeler Ministry

How did Jesus evict
a thousand and one
unwanted house guests?
Plant your finger softly
onto lips and press.
Slowly blow breath
through puckered lips.
And there you have it:
the classic
French gesture
for "Shusshhh!"
Don't let gentleness
fool you for a moment.
Those demons are
out of here!
Distant relatives
of the cat family
sporting nine
(count them) lives.
All conveniently
found on the
enneagram.

God makes promises
and keeps them.
God's Word's as good
as any written contract.
(Jesus Christ:
it better be.)

Like timid Conrads
we stammer:
"Are you sure?"
And with patient
Berger-like persistence
God responds:
"Count on it!"

Jesus dismisses
a whole missaletted
congregation of
howling voices,
(from within and
of course without)
that keep us from
hearing,
embracing,
and sharing
our stories.

Visitors, like fish,
smell after three days.
And so,
in no uncertain terms,
he dismisses
all those strangers
that came for a visit
and decided to stay.
Their constantly
distracting presence
closes eyes,
stops up ears,
hardens not just
arteries
but hearts,
keeps us from
amening the

timeless twisted
tales of others.

*   *   *

Conversion: To wholeness and healing.

Scripture: "As Jesus was getting into the boat, the man who had been possessed begged to be allowed to stay with him. Jesus would not let him but said to him, 'Go home to your people and tell them all that the Lord in his mercy has done for you.' So the man went off and proceeded to spread throughout the Decapolis all that Jesus had done for him. And everyone was amazed." [Mark 5:18–20]

One Good Sneeze Deserves Another

Isn't it funny
how you find
help,
direction,
nurture,
"good news,"
where you least
expect it?

The desert
bristles with
quiet life.
Everywhere
unlooked for clues,
(with the urgency
of an untrained toddler
looking for a rest
room)
ready to burst
into bloom.
Life,
in all her forms,
the quintessential
Beatitude.

This afternoon,
warm sea, cool breeze,
wet sand and white waves
usher me into
pelican school.

They teach more than
a thing or two.

Instead of soaring high,
swooping,
diving knifelike
through the moving
wetness for a
midafternoon meal,
they just sit there.
They know a good thing
when they see it,
when they taste it.

Five sly,
sky diving,
broad beaked birds
floating there
not the least bit
anxious
to move on.
Poking here,
gulping there,
untold tidy morsels
to be found
in these calm and
common waters.

Lots to feed upon.
Their necks nodding,
their actions
a thousand times
more eloquent than
bird brained blabberings,
they seem to say:
"Keep digging,
dingbats,
there's more
where that came from."

Inexhaustible riches
found only
in the deserts
of land and sea
and words:
Beatitude.

*   *   *

Conversion: To treasure life-giving questions.

Scripture: "Happy are those who hunger and thirst for what is right: they shall be satisfied." [Matthew 5:6]

Spring Cleaning

O God who wants
our wholeness,
you lead the wounded
to water you cannot
make them drink.
Self-inflicted fragmentations
only make you flinch.
What keeps
your healing power
from what it can do?
Is it "who" or "what"
that constantly
short-circuits
this paschal process?

Feelings are angels,
messengers of God,
that give us
easily ignored information
about everything we ever
wanted to know about life
but were afraid to ask.

Listen to feelings.
Stop treating them
like hostile aliens
from another galaxy.
Stop the fighting,
denying and criticizing.
What are we afraid
we'll hear

about ourselves,
others,
who we are,
where we've been,
where we're going?
Instead of asking
questions that are
"Not A Through Street,"
questions that
do not explore or
investigate but
soundly condemn,
(Questions like
"Why am I having
these feeling?"
Judgments of their
implied goodness
or, more often the case,
their badness.)
Try a refreshingly
different approach,
the new sparkling flavor of
"What do you want to tell me?"

✳   ✳   ✳

Conversion: Learning to value the feelings of our heart.

Scripture: "But a Samaritan traveler (a foreigner) who came upon him was moved with compassion when he saw him." [Luke 10:33]

Distant Relations

Where are our deserted spaces?
Where are our uncluttered places
of play and rest and prayer?
Do we ever vacation there?
What do we take
on such short notice?
Spontaneous excursions
always catch us unprepared.

How do you feed
five thousand guests
that decide to stay
for dinner?
The Teacher's heart is
moved by all he sees.
He lets this hurting
hungry heap of humanity
transform him into
maitre d'.

Each walking wound
a story of search and struggle
for that wholeness
just beyond their grasp.
Hell.
At this point
they'd settle for halfness.
That's ten times more
than what they have.

It's getting late.
We're cold.
We're hungry.
This is about
as much fun as
being on a safari
without a guide.
Lots of dangerous things
out here.
We're lost in a maze
of grace.
So what's for dinner?
God knows
it must be better than
the countless cans of emptiness
we've feasted on before.

Whatever happened to truth
in advertising?
Remember those inflated
tantalizing offers of products
that promised more
than they could deliver?
It all comes down
to supply and demand.
You cannot ever give
what you've never ever had.
So, what's for dinner?
Yeah. And my friend here
wants to know
what's for dessert?

❋　　　❋　　　❋

Conversion:　**To taking, blessing, breaking and sharing what we
have and are.**

Scripture: "When evening came, the disciples went to him and said, 'This is a lonely place, and the time has slipped by; so send the people away, and they can go to the villages to buy themselves some food.' Jesus replied, 'There is no need for them to go: give them something to eat yourselves.' " [Matthew 14:15–16]

Proper Dents

Beginning,
planning,
plotting,
spotting
defensive softness,
always jockeying,
for that
advantageous position.

Meet the Monty Hall
of discernment.
He looks much smaller
and more manageable
on the tube.
He greets us with
his patented:
"Let's make a deal."
Hurried, worried looks
meet his offer
as we wrestle with
what might be
the "right" decision.
Two doors and one curtain.
Certain two will disappoint
and one reward.
Bumper car introspection
always leaves those
telltale marks

like nicks in
new paint.

We interrupt this poem
for a special news brief.
I don't know
if you're quite ready
for this.
We have just
received word from
a reliable source
who wishes
to remain anonymous.
It doesn't matter
which you choose.
The payoff?
You never lose
except by choosing
not to play.
Fear will paralyze you,
make you impotent
to risk,
to trust,
to choose.
For you see
whatever,
whichever,
whoever,
whenever,
wherever,
however
you choose,
(And here's the
Grand Prize Payoff)
"I am" with you.
Surprise?

No.
Providence.
So,
what's your pleasure?
Which will it be?

Film at eleven.

＊   ＊   ＊

Conversion: To making life-giving choices.

Scripture: "I set before you life and death, blessing or curse. Choose life, then, so that you and your descendants may live." [Deuteronomy 30:19]

Contemporary Annotations

by Steve Privett, S.J.

1. Pay careful attention
   to "peripheral" concerns
   or so-called distractions.
   Note that Jesus spent
   lots of time and energy
   trying to convince folks that
   whom/what they considered peripheral
   was at the heart of the matter.

2. Hindsight—
   and only hindsight—
   is 20/20.
   The most accurate perspective
   on life
   is from the other side
   of death.
   The only way
   to see things
   as they really are
   is by dying.
   What a bummer!

3. For the person of "common sense,"
   God's wisdom is simply foolishness;
   Jesus, for example.
   Maybe God—
   and only God—
   can "save" us all.

4. "Much is expected
   from those to whom
   much has been given." [Luke 12:49]

We have been given the same Word,
graced by the same Spirit
and nourished at the same table as
Oscar Romero, Rutillio Grande,
Ita Ford, Dorothy Kazel,
Jeanne Donovan and Maura Clark.

Indwelling

First Prediction.
"If you want
to come after me,
deny yourself,
take up your cross
and follow
in my footsteps."

We come to know
a Master's moves
by dwelling in his acts.
Piece together
this paschal puzzle
with Lao Tzu's words
haunting us as we go.
A journey
of three thousand miles
begun with one step.
Where will it lead?
Each one's cross,
each one's passion,
each one's crucifixion
shows signs of
dermal similarity,
epidermal uniqueness.

Second Prediction.
"The Son of Man
will be delivered,
die and rise.
Although they did not

understand his words,
they were afraid
to question him."

Convenient density.
Thick by choice
not by nature.
Reticence
the product
of intuitional fear.
No need to have
our worst suspicions
confirmed.
So we play dumb,
attempt to conceal
we know precisely
what he means.
In these security
briefings,
why must he
take the tact
of worst scenarios?

Third Prediction.
"Unless you turn
and become like children,
you will never enter
the kingdom of God."

"If you perceive
my meaning."
Why must he always
speak in metaphor?
Why not say
what he means?
Learners on a road
going up to
(clear to some
muddy to others)
Jerusalem.

Our mood,
as constant
as the stars,
was mild confusion.
Those who
know him less
and followed
further back
were brave enough
to feel the tug
of failing nerves.
Like Bob and Bing,
in good old days,
we sang and
danced our way
"On the Road to
Redemption."

✳   ✳   ✳

Conversion: To follow Christ in the Paschal Mystery.

Scripture: "The language of the cross may be illogical to those who are not on the way to salvation, but those of us who are on the way see it as God's power to save. . . . For God's foolishness is wiser than human wisdom, and God's weakness is stronger than human strength." [1 Corinthians 1:18,25]

Good Old Paschal School Days

A man of few
well chosen words
and chiseled actions.
A masterful methodology:
experience it,
chew on it,
then spit it out
in convincing deed.
Let your life
break open
its meaning
and your memory
keep the spirit
of mimetic magnanimity
burning like an
everlasting beacon
through imitation.

Curious if we know
what he just did for us.
Gave us an example.
We're supposed to do
what he has done.
What I'd give
for some plain talk!

Teacher to the end.
No worries
if you forget
the words, mate.
Recall the gesture.

Remember:
there's a story buried
deep in every action.
While it may cause
a squirm or two,
it contains the germ
of transfiguration.
Catch it.
It's terminal.
Keep asking the question.
What is the story?
What's the meaning
of a teacher washing
dirty learners' feet?
Something to chew on
when you find
yourselves together
for another meal.

So we'll be happy
if we take what
he's just said
and put it
into practice?
That's the problem.
The big "if."
Amazing, isn't it?
This character
hides nothing.
This guy plays poker
with his cards facing us.
We're not used to this.
Our minds keep buzzing:
"What's his game?
What's his angle?"
So simple
So clear.
So brief.

So bare.
Scarry stuff here.

*   *   *

Conversion: To imitate the example of Christ in serving our brothers and sisters.

Scripture: "I have given you an example so that you may copy what I have done to you. . . . Now that you know this, happiness will be yours if you behave accordingly." [John 13:15,17]

Table Talk

"During the meal . . ."

Think of all the wonderful
things that happen
during a meal.

Bread of remembrance?
Cup of blessing?
How are we blessed
huddled in this
upper room?
What do we remember
as we anxiously await
impending doom?
What images come unbidden
through the actions
we perform?
Follow that succession
of faces and places.
Memory's joggers,
in the midst of routine
ritual repetition,
become unaccountably
present epiphanies.

"After singing songs of praise,
they walked out to the garden."

We face that phantom
paschal fear,
the paradox of
life through death,

with a song in our heart
and a lump in our throat.
We pray for no melodic
miscarriages today.

All those ominous clues,
catastrophic events
continue to unfold
against the shadow
of the cross
(just over the horizon there)
lurking ever-present
in restless imaginations.
How do we look past
the pain
and actions
that squeeze the very
life out of you
to a paschal resolution?

How does one distinguish
between betrayals?
Two traitors here.
Why is one cursed
while the other is
ultimately blessed
by all who remember
these deeds done
centuries ago?
Perhaps you always
liked him better.

Denial and betrayal.
Betrayer denies
the possibility
of forgiveness.
Denier betrays
a friend
but not the power
of love

to heal and mend.
He stumbles
with unkept promises
into a fetal
Pauline intuition:
"Nothing can
separate us from
the love of God."

They are different,
then,
not in deed
but consequence.
Both
confounding
infidelities
of a friend.

* * *

Conversion: Belief in God's unbounded love.

Scripture: "For I am certain of this: neither death nor life, no angel, no prince, nothing that exists, nothing still to come, not any power, or height or depth, nor any created thing, can ever come between us and the love of God made visible in Christ Jesus our Lord." [Romans 8:38–39]

Last Days' Epitaph

Elisha said:
"I pray you,
let me inherit
a double portion
of your spirit."
Elijah replied:
"You have asked
a hard thing."
    [2 Kings 2:9–10]

[Inside]

Travel light.
Carry nothing
that will
burden you
or weigh you
down.

Do not
bludgeon people
with your faith.
Do not
inflict your wisdom
on the weary.
A timely
cup of water
can be more prophetic

than all
your platitudes.

People
deflect,
neglect
your words.
Actions are
infectious.
There is no antidote.
Once touched
by the disease
then learn
to love it.
It can keep you
healthy.

[Outside]

Nameless vigilantes
armed for combat
needing no details
of how or why
this evening sport
was born,
just hoping
for some conflict.

Dead or alive
is all the same
to them.
Unbridled power
is like
a pit bull
on a broken leash.

There's always
room for more.
Invite a friend.

* * *

Conversion: To let what we believe be seen in the actions of our life.

Scripture: "The community of those who believed shared all things in common." [Acts 2:44]

Objects in the Mirror Are Closer Than You Think

Pleasant progress,
as unplanned journeys go,
until we meet the sign:
"Road under construction."
Could have fooled me.
Everything torn up
in marvelous disarray.
Earmarks of destruction
to uneducated eyes.

Simply put:
No getting around it.
Only one way through.
Penetrate the pain
and find the presence.

Passion?
Only this:
to stay with you
in your pain.
Reject the Western bias
for practicality.
Refuse to quickly
cover nakedness
or turn away
my blood flushed cheeks.

Mind sputtering
like an old computer
on a cold morning.

Frantically,
I punch up menu.
What can I do?
What can I say?
Searching for some
"s" word:
"sorry," "surely," "so."
All dull swords
against the face
of this unfolding
tragedy.
Afraid to face
impending impotence.
Will I, too,
run away?

   ✳   ✳   ✳

Conversion: **The courage to accept human frailty and weakness.**

Scripture: **"My grace is enough for you; my great strength is revealed in weakness." [2 Corinthians 12:9]**

Two-Sided Coins

Two scenes,
contrasting themes,
each the woof and warp
of the other.
The first: accusations.
The second: denials.
Each containing
partial truths
twisted
beyond
recognition.

Jesus
like a stand-up comic
on opening night
among strangers:
a hostile audience this.
Just your average,
blood-thirsty,
home-town crowd.
Graciousness no part
of their "welcome" repertoire.

A trial
that took place
under cover
of night.
Strange deliberations.
Justice
was not served
in these proceedings.

Scripture was.
Small consolation
for the accused
and condemned.

Why do cowards
seem so brave
at night?
Why does truth
radiate
under scrutiny?
More passion paradoxes
leading to that
paschal thing.

* * *

Conversion: To truthful words and actions.

Scripture: "If you make my word your home
you will indeed be my disciples,
you will learn the truth
and the truth will make you free." [John 8:31–32]

Contemporary Annotations

by Leo Rock, S.J.

3. *God's Ways Are Not Our Ways*

How is this
for the understatement
of all time:
"God's ways are not
our ways."

I planned for sunshine.
It was inexorably
foggy.

I expected
grinding teeth
and enduring it.
I enjoyed it.

I sought answers
to all those questions.
I found, instead,
new questions
which made the old
obsolete.

I thought this was
a wrapping up,
an ending,
a completion.
It is,
to my complete surprise,
another beginning.

4. *So What?!*

Usually with a bit of a snarl,
At least a curled lip.
A dismissal, a put down.
Irony.

How sad, so vital a question,
So life-offering a question
Is reduced to serving
Irony.

You are loved and cherished,
More than you can dare to imagine,
By God.
So what?

God, incredibly,
needs your help
To bring the Kingdom of God
To earth.
So what?

Peace, love, joy
Are the gifts of
God's Spirit.
So what?

Do you see what I mean?

Witness for the Prosecution

No thundering
theophany here.
No, more like
the gentleness
that sneaks up on us
like summer fog
at sunset.

What is undeniable
is the fact
that he was there.
A few brief hours before
he was leader of the pack.
They scattered,
splintered off in
twelve directions
by the impact
of one giant agate
on an unsuspecting cluster.
Tarnished
discipleship
quickly lost
its luster.

Time now, however,
to regroup.
So here he was,
a contingent
following
of one.
And even this

solitary
sentry
was waffling
under pressure.

A second
indisputable fact:
he "spilled the beans"
on himself.
These are the days
before "Plumbers"
and paper shredders:
all those finger-tip
convenient ways
to dispose of
momentary indiscretions.

He could have glossed
this over easily.
He didn't.
Why does he refuse
to exorcise imperfection?
Why not erase
forever
this momentary lapse
of concentration,
this minuscule speck
on an otherwise
impeccable record?

When you're up
to your neck
in alligators,
what difference
will one more make?
The Defense rests.

✳   ✳   ✳

Conversion: **To the love of God given to us in the midst of human suffering.**

Scripture: "For God says: 'At the favorable time, I have listened to you; on the day of salvation I came to your help.' Well, now is the favorable time; this is the day of salvation . . . we prove we are the servants of God by great fortitude in times of suffering: in times of hardship and distress." [2 Corinthians 6:2,4]

Convicting Truth

What a difference
six days make.
The metamorphosis
of palm waving
hosannas
into fist clenching
Barabbases.
Go with the flow?

A week ago they would
have made you king.
You could have ridden
a wave of popularity
into power.
Today
the tide is
out.
You'll be lucky
to get out
of this town
in one piece.

❋   ❋   ❋

Conversion: Confidence in the midst of trials.

Scripture: "When we are made to suffer, it is for your consolation and salvation. When, instead, we are com-

forted, this should be a consolation to you, supporting you in patiently bearing the same sufferings as we bear. And our hope for you is confident, since we know that, sharing our sufferings, you will also share our consolations." [2 Corinthians 1:6–7]

Decaffeinated Questions

"Who will roll away the stone?"
As morning darkness
slowly lifts,
before a rooster's
cleared his throat,
when normal people
enjoy the warmth
provided by
the blanket
or body
next to them,
three friends make
their grief-crazed way
toward the edge of town.
The trip, the tasks, the tears,
touched by memory
of these past three days,
all ritual gestures
of leave-taking.
This is how love
struggles to say
"good-bye."

"Who will roll away the stone?"
How many thoughts aborted,
how many feelings still-born,
how many dreams deserted,
imaginations orphaned
by the weight of this
solitary question?

Their pace and faces set,
their direction clear.
They will not turn back.
Friendship all they have
to fight cold logic's opposition.
"We'll cross that bridge
when we come to it."

The first of many paradoxes
on the other side
of these paschal events.
Who would have thought
the stones we stumbled over
would form the bridge
to all that lies beyond?

✳   ✳   ✳

Conversion: To live in the hope of the resurrection.

Scripture: "These sufferings bring patience, as we know, and patience brings perseverance, and perseverance brings hope, and this hope is not deceptive, because the love of God has been poured into our hearts by the Holy Spirit which has been given to us." [Romans 5:4–5]

On the Road to Epiphanies

We are
traveling storytellers
who sift through the rubble
of ruined dreams.
So much hope
crushed.
So much promise
unfulfilled.
The image of
three empty crosses
against the far horizon
burns in our memories.
Haunted,
as we walk,
by this
and news
of an empty tomb.

Blinded by this rascal
paschal paralysis,
we cannot see
the tip of our tongue,
the end of our nose,
the pattern cooler heads
just might perceive.

If things weren't bad enough,
some stranger barges in,
from God knows where,
and wants us to repeat
our studied lamentations.

Aware we have an audience,
two fresh open ears,
we dive back into
our tale of tragedy.

And then he has the nerve
to gently chide us.
"Don't mistake
the end of a chapter
for the end of the story."
What kind of crazy caveat
do his words convey?
A strange sense of déjà vu:
he turns a phrase the way
the Teacher did.

Invited to explain,
his eyes, his images,
his tone of voice,
all slowly cast a spell
and light a fire
in that small still place
deep within us all.

✳   ✳   ✳

Conversion: To live lives built on Christian remembrance (*Story*) and thanksgiving (*Eucharist*).

Scripture: "Then they said to each other, 'Did not our hearts burn within us as he talked to us on the road and explained the scriptures to us?' . . . Then they told their story of what had happened on the road and how they had recognized him in the breaking of the bread." [Luke 24:32,35]

Ah Yes, I Remember It Well

Early morning
fish fry.
Eat and meet.
Eyes are opened
as stomachs are filled.
And then an old
Italian custom.
A little stroll
along the beach
to help the
indigestion.

Why do teachers
repeat themselves?
Ask me once.
I might forget.
Ask me twice.
I might even blush.
Ask me three times
and I just might remember.

Children never tire
of asking the same questions
over and over again.
Each repetition
invites the
interrogated learner
to push further
into the mystery
that it points to.

Teacher to the end.
Repetition mothers learning.
Memory births wisdom.
Cherish burning questions.
They always lead to life.

✳   ✳   ✳

Conversion: To learn how to treasure life-giving questions.

Scripture: "Then he said to him a third time, 'Simon, son of John, do you love me?' Peter was upset that he asked him a third time, 'Do you love me?' and said, 'Lord, you know everything; you know that I love you.' Jesus said to him, 'Feed my sheep.' " [John 21:17]

Litany of Contradictory Things

Wheat and weeds:
let them grow together.
Arabs and Jews in Palestine:
let them grow together.
Greeks and Turks of the Balkans:
let them grow together.
Catholics and Protestants
of Northern Ireland:
let them grow together.
Pros and Contras
of Central America:
let them grow together.
Documented and undocumented aliens:
let them grow together.
Immigrants and Native Americans:
let them grow together.
Blacks and Whites
of South Africa:
let them grow together.
Siks and Hindus of India:
let them grow together.
Revolutionaries and reactionaries:
let them grow together.
Russians and Americans:
let them grow together.
Gorbachev and Reagan and
all leaders of the world:
let them grow together.
Religious leaders who

lay and lighten burdens:
let them grow together.
Disciples prone
to boasts and betrayals:
let them grow together.
People of God
who wound and heal:
let them grow together.
Rich and poor, humble and haughty:
let them grow together.
Those whose thinking
is similar and contrary:
let them grow together.
Those whose feelings
are transparent or concealed:
let them grow together.
Days of sparseness
and days of plenty:
let them grow together.
Winter, spring, summer, fall:
let them grow together.
All the seasons of one's life:
let them grow together.
Joys and sorrow, laughter, tears:
let them grow together.
Passion and death,
resurrection and new life:
let them grow together.
Comfort and challenge:
let them grow together.
Strength and weakness:
let them grow together
Doubt and faith:
let them grow together.
Denial and commitment:
let them grow together.
Preoccupation and freedom:
let them grow together.

Virtue and vice:
let them grow together.
Contemplation and action:
let them grow together.
Giving and receiving:
let them grow together.
The helpful and the helpless:
let them grow together.
Wisdom of the East and West:
let them grow together.
All contrarities of the Lord:
let them grow together.

✳   ✳   ✳

Conversion: To embrace and celebrate the paradoxes and apparent contradictions in life.

Scripture: "They asked him: 'Do you want us to go and pull up the weeds?' He told them: 'No, when you pull up the weeds, you might take the wheat along with them. Let them just grow together until harvest.' " [Matthew 13:29–30]

Epilogue

This book has been a long time coming. Nine years to be exact. The Society of Jesus of the California Province asked me to work in our Novitiate from 1973–1976. During those three years I had the chance to pray, reflect, imagine and write. Two collections of Prayer-Poems were the fruit of those three fertile years. *God of Untold Tales*[1] was the first collection. *God of Seasons*[2] was the second.

I wrote those prayer poems as a way of capturing some of the movements of the Spirit in my own faith journey. I was surprised and heartened to realize that they spoke to others who were struggling to discover the dwelling places of God in their own life.

As I traveled and taught over the next eight years in such marvelous places as Australia, Korea, Japan, Canada and the United States, I met with the same bewildering question from those who had read the first two collections: "When are you going to write some more prayer-poems?" I often wondered that myself. In order to do it, I knew I needed two things: time and quiet.

St. Ignatius of Loyola, the founder of the Jesuits, followed a spiritual path that combined contemplation with action. To ensure that those who followed after him in the Society of Jesus would be called to integrate both of these elements in their life and ministry, he had the wisdom to suggest that part of a Jesuit's formation would be Tertianship.

Tertianship is a period of time that comes at the end of a Jesuit's training when he has finished studies and has been engaged in active ministry. It is referred to, at times, as a "school of the heart."[3]

Most people engage in the Tertianship experience some three to five years after ordination. This would be around their thirteenth to fifteenth year in the Society of Jesus. Partly because of my gypsy-like ministerial peregrinations, partly because of my affection for and identification with Martha over Mary in the gospels, I successfully delayed Tertianship until my twenty-fifth year in the Society of Jesus.

Two of the gifts of Tertianship for me were time and quiet. During the two summers (1987 and 1988) and the intervening year, I had a chance to rest, relax, pray, reflect, remember, imagine, integrate and write. This was an amazing and grace-filled time for me and the thirteen other Jesuits who accompanied me on this stage of our faith journey.

An image I had throughout this entire experience was that of a small child gently crying. The child was everything I had heard and learned but forgotten. The child was everything I needed in order to preserve and nurture life in me and around me instead of foolishly squandering or destroying it. The child was that in me and each of us that we desperately need for peace, healing, wholeness and survival on our planet. That child is *Orphaned Wisdom.*

The prayer poems themselves came out of my experience of the thirty day retreat during the first summer of Tertianship. I was able to creatively brood over them during the year that followed that experience. I was able to give them final shape during my second summer of Tertianship. I am grateful to the staff and community of the Jesuit Novitiate in Santa Barbara for their hospitality and good humor which helped me enormously with this creative project.

I wish to offer special thanks to Leo Rock, Jack Boyle and Tom McCormick who were our Tertian Directors. Their gentle humor and timely homiletic insight was used effectively by the Spirit on more than one occasion.

I also wish to thank three fellow Tertians who live and work with me at Santa Clara University. Curtis Bryant, Sonny Manuel, and Steve Privett have joined Leo Rock and myself in creating contemporary annotations for those engaged in the spiritual life. These appear on the Sundays of each week. A cursory reading of them will reveal how different we all are.

These contemporary annotations are small pieces of wisdom, a smorgasbord of advice for pilgrims on their spiritual journey. They suggest a variety of ways one can look for and unexpectedly find the dwelling places of God among us. If they articulate some small part of your experience of the spiritual life, use them and remember them. If they don't articulate your experience of the spiritual life, don't use them and don't remember them. It's as simple as that.

Finally, if you find the prayer-poems in *Orphaned Wisdom* helpful, why not share them with a friend? If you don't find them helpful, why not share them with an enemy? Sharing always pleased my mother. And remember: God works in strange and wonderful ways.

NOTES

1. *God of Untold Tales* by Michael E. Moynahan, S.J. (San Jose: Resource Publications, Inc., 1979).

2. *God of Seasons* by Michael E. Moynahan, S.J. (San Jose: Resource Publications, Inc., 1980).

3. *The Constitutions of the Society of Jesus,* translated by George E. Ganss, S.J. (St. Louis: The Institute of Jesuit Resources, 1970), p. 234.